Understanding Sound

Horatio Mendez

Infomax Readers

Rosen Classroom™

New York

Published in 2014 by The Rosen Publishing Group, Inc.
29 East 21st Street, New York, NY 10010

Book Design: Mickey Harmon

Photo Credits: Cover Edwin Verin/Shutterstock.com; p. 5 wavebreakmedia/Shutterstock.com; p. 7 (lightning) 2009fotofriends/Shutterstock.com; p. 7 (fireworks) Wesley Guijt/Shutterstock.com; p. 9 Galushko Sergey/Shutterstock.com; p. 11 (ear) ArTono/Shutterstock.com; p. 11 (eardrum) Oguz Aral/Shutterstock.com; p. 13 Andrew Oischer/Shutterstock.com; p. 15 Tadas_Naujokaitis78/Shutterstock.com; p. 17 Gelpi/Shutterstock.com; p. 19 Willyam Bradberry/Shutterstock.com; p. 21 (vocal cord) hkannn/Shutterstock.com; p. 21 (mouth) mathom/Shutterstock.com.

ISBN: 978-1-4777-2393-7
6-pack ISBN: 978-1-4777-2394-4

Manufactured in the United States of America

CPSIA Compliance Information: Batch #CS13RC: For further information contact Rosen Publishing, New York, New York at 1-800-237-9932.

Contents

What Is Sound?

You may know that many different objects make sound. You may also know that we use our ears to hear. But have you ever thought about the science behind sound?

Sound waves are all around us, but they're invisible. That means we can't see them. Even though we can't see sound waves, they're a huge part of our everyday lives.

These kids are hearing sound waves through their headphones.

Sound is a form of **energy** that we can hear. There are many kinds of energy, such as light, heat, and sound. We see, feel, and hear these energies all the time.

Different energies travel at different speeds. Light travels faster than sound, so light energy reaches us before sound energy does. That's why we see lightning before we hear thunder during a thunderstorm.

When we see fireworks,
we see the lights before we hear the boom.

Sound Waves

Many objects make noise, but not all the time. Sound only happens when an object vibrates. When something vibrates, it moves back and forth very quickly.

When an object vibrates, it pushes around tiny pieces of matter in the air, called molecules (MAH-lih-kyoolz). The molecules push into other molecules and form sound waves. Then, the sound waves travel to our ears.

When you hit the top of a drum with a drumstick, the drum vibrates and creates sound.

When a sound wave reaches us, it enters our ears. Then it hits our eardrums.

When the eardrum vibrates, it moves tiny bones that send messages to the **brain**. Then, the brain works to tell us what kind of sound it is. The brain is so smart that it can tell the difference between many kinds of sounds.

We call the tiny, thin piece of skin an eardrum because it looks like the top of a drum!

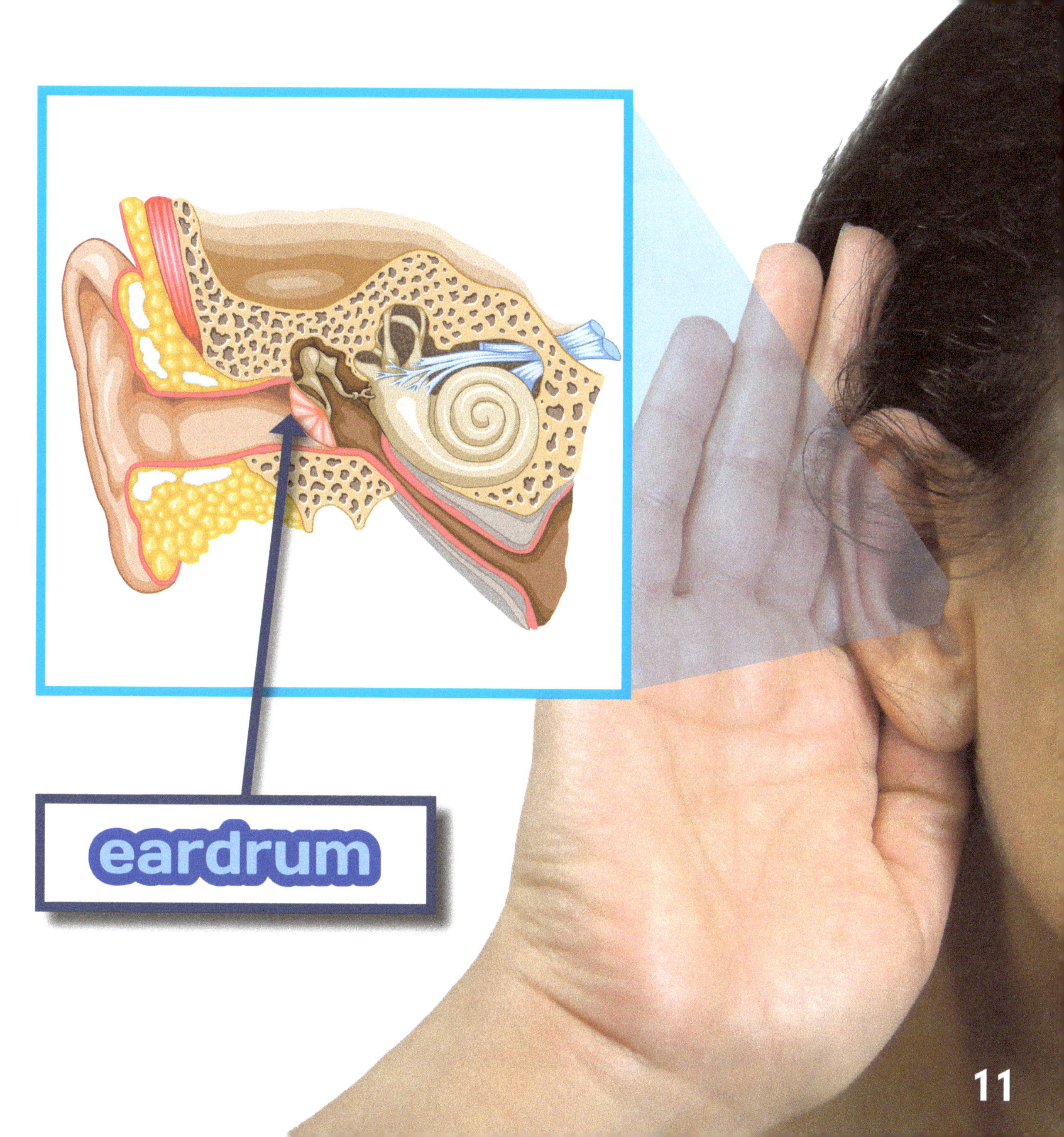
eardrum

Loud Sounds, Soft Sounds

We measure sound in several different ways. One way is through volume. Volume tells us how loud or soft a sound is. Loud sounds have a lot of energy. Soft sounds only have a little energy.

We can hear loud sounds without being close to the **source** of the sounds. Their waves have enough energy to carry them far away. That's why you can hear a fire truck without being near it.

Firefighters and police officers have to be careful the sirens don't hurt their ears!

F.D.N.Y.
F.D.
N.Y.
E 9
Fresh Food!

High and Low

We also measure sound through pitch. A sound's pitch can be high or low. Pitch is caused by how fast something vibrates. Fast vibrations make high-pitched sounds, while slow vibrations make low-pitched sounds.

You can think about pitch by picturing the strings on a guitar. When you play a high note, the string vibrates very fast. When you play a low note, the string vibrates more slowly.

A guitar has six strings. They vibrate when you pluck them, making many different sounds.

Now that you understand what sound is, you can understand how it moves. Sound waves can move through solids, liquids, and gases. But sometimes sound waves can be blocked or **absorbed**.

When you close a window or use earplugs, you stop sound waves from reaching your ears. Receiving fewer sound waves makes the sound seem quieter.

It's important to take care of our hearing. We can hurt our ears if we hear too many loud sounds.

What Are Echoes?

Have you ever heard an echo? An echo happens when sound waves bounce off an object and return to where they came from.

Dolphins, bats, and other animals use echoes to move around and find food. This is called **echolocation**. The sound waves hit an object, such as a tasty fish, and come back to them. This tells them where the object is.

Echolocation helps dolphins find their food underwater.

Sound Is Everywhere

People make sounds just like animals and objects do. It happens when our **vocal cords** vibrate. The next time you talk, put your hands on your throat. It's cool to feel where sound comes from!

Sound is important to our everyday lives. It lets us hear our favorite music and talk to other people. Sound is a big part of understanding what and where things are in the world around us!

You can feel the vibrations in your throat when you talk or sing.

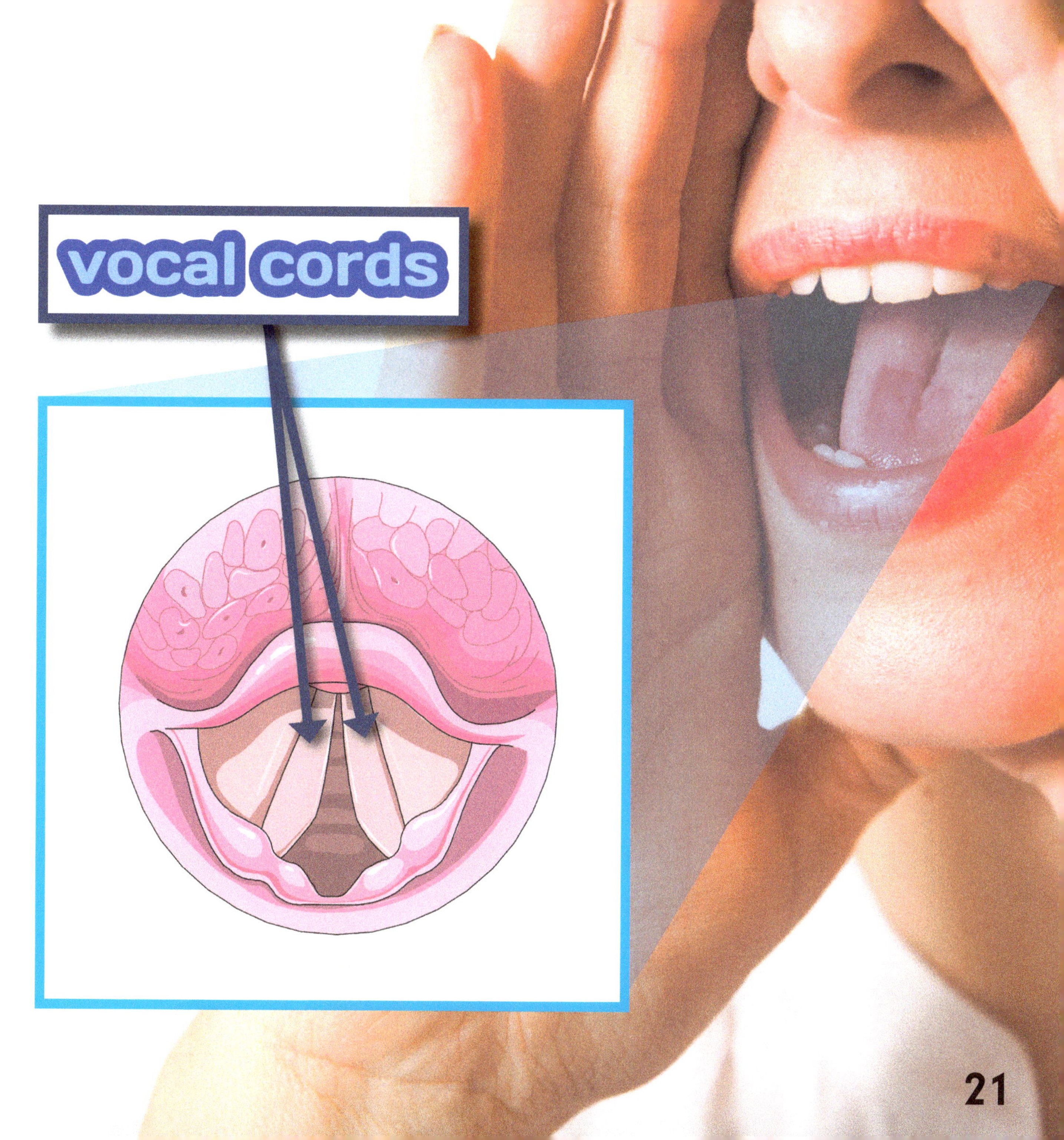
vocal cords

All About Sound!

Can you tell the difference between the sounds listed below?

volume	
loud	soft
lion's roar siren scream	mouse's squeak wind whisper

pitch	
high	low
a baby's cry whistle a bird singing	an adult man's voice bass drum tiger's growl

Glossary

absorb (uhb-ZOHRB) To take in.

brain (BRAYN) The organ in the head that controls the body.

echolocation (eh-koh-loh-KAY-shun) The use of sound to find food and locate objects.

energy (EH-nurh-jee) The ability to do work.

source (SORS) The place where something begins.

vocal cords (VOH-kuhl KOHRDZ) Tissues in the throat that vibrate and make noise when air passes over them, allowing us to speak.

Index